CONTENTS

MEASURING ELECTRICITY

Four times a year, most homes in Britain get an **electricity** bill. The more electricity you use, the more you have to pay.

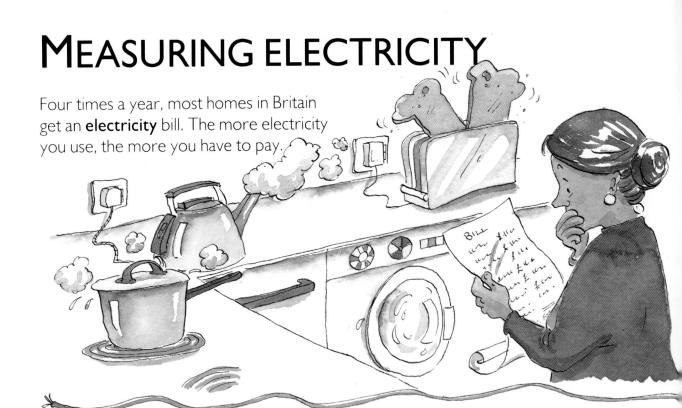

Switching on a light allows an electrical current to flow in your home and through the lightbulb. The more lights and other electrical things that are switched on in your home, the more electricity is used.

As it enters your home, the electrical current flows through a meter which keeps a record of the amount of electricity you have used.

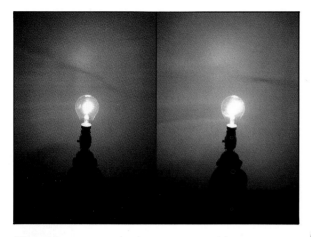

This is the amount of electricity people use in different countries. This list shows how many 100 watt lightbulbs each person would have burning all the time.

Electric power isn't measured in grams, metres or litres but in watts. Here are two electric lightbulbs that look pretty much alike but the numbers on the top show that they use different amounts of power. The one on the right uses 100 watts of electrical power. If you kept that lightbulb switched on for 10 hours, you would use about 10 pence worth or electricity. The 40 watt bulb uses less electrical power: it would cost about 4 pence for the same length of time.

A 100 watt lightbulb is more expensive. Why do you think a person would choose to use one?

100 people share 1	Cambodia
50 people share 1	Ethiopia
25 people share 1	Uganda
10 people share 1	Bangladesh
5 people share 1	Kenya
3 people share 1	India
2 people share 1	China
1	Egypt
1	Jamaica
1½	Malaysia
1½	Mexico
2	Argentina
5	Italy
6½	United Kingdom
7½	Japan
7½	France
10	Australia
13	United States
21	Canada
28	Norway

Wow!

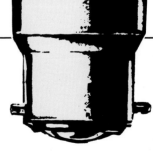

People in Britain use enough electricity in a year to keep more than 350,000,000 100 watt lightbulbs burning for a year.

BATTERIES

Here are some of the **battery**-powered things that you and your family might use. How many more can you think of?

Have you ever found that something has stopped working because it needs new batteries?

When you change batteries you need to have batteries that are the right size and shape.

Don't try to open a battery – what is inside is poisonous.

If you can get a good look inside the place where the batteries go, you will see that at each end of the battery holder is a piece of metal or a metal spring that must touch the end batteries to make a **circuit**.

Electricity from a battery costs about 1000 times as much as electricity from the mains.

You also have to put them in the right way round or they won't work.

This is how a battery works

Inside a battery is a kind of chemical sandwich. Two different chemicals are separated from each other by a layer of damp paste.

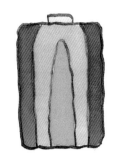

When you make a circuit that connects one end of the battery to the other end, the two chemicals begin to change into new chemicals. As they change, an electrical current flows along the circuit from one chemical to the other.

As long as the circuit connects the two ends of the battery, the current will flow and the two chemicals will keep changing.

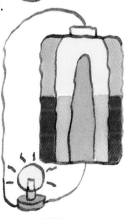

When the two chemicals have completely changed the current stops – the batteries have run out.

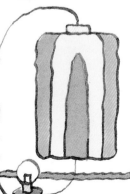

DISCOVERING ELECTRICITY

If you have ever turned on a light, watched television or played with a **battery**-operated toy, then you have made **electricity** work for you.

Two hundred years ago people had no idea that electricity could do work or be useful in any way. In fact, two hundred years ago, only the world's most brilliant scientists had even heard of electricity and they were very puzzled by it.

They had invented machines which made tiny flashes of lightning as they turned the handle. This seemed to have something to do with electricity.

They had also discovered that if they touched a lightning machine as it flashed they would get a shock.

The scientists continued to work away trying to understand the puzzle of electricity but the more they worked the more of a puzzle it seemed to be.

An Italian named Alessandro Volta found a completely new way of producing electricity in 1800. He put together many layers of two metals called zinc and copper, and separated them with soggy paste board. A current of electricity seemed to flow from the bottom to the top. No one knew it at the time, but Volta had made the first battery.

Volta makes the first battery.

Then, in 1831, an English scientist named Michael Faraday discovered a way to make an electrical current flow with the help of a magnet. He first did this by spinning a metal disc between the two ends of a magnet. He found that an electrical current flowed along a wire that was touching the metal disc.

Michael Faraday produces an electrical current

This discovery made scientists realize that electricity was more than just an interesting puzzle. They saw that it might be possible to produce an electrical current that could drive machinery and perhaps do other useful work. Do you think Michael Faraday would be surprised if he saw all the things that electricity does today?

Make a list of everything that works by battery. Think how you would manage without them.

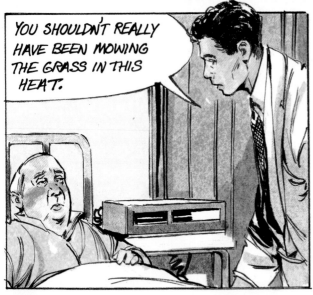

RESUSCITATION

STRUCK BY LIGHTNING!

IT'S CHARGED

STAND BACK!

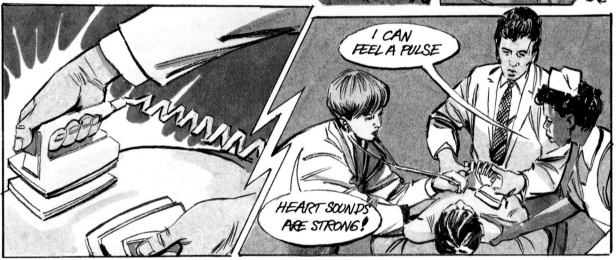

I CAN FEEL A PULSE

HEART SOUNDS ARE STRONG!

DOCTORS CAN SOMETIMES GET A HEART THAT HAS STOPPED BEATING TO START AGAIN USING SPECIAL EQUIPMENT. AN ELECTRICAL CURRENT FLOWING THROUGH THE HEART SEEMS TO JOLT IT BACK INTO BEATING PROPERLY.

IF A PATIENT'S HEART HAS BEEN DAMAGED BY HEART DISEASE IT MAY NOT START AGAIN BUT THIS BOY'S HEART WAS PERFECTLY NORMAL.

HE'S A VERY LUCKY BOY.

9

THEY DO IT WITH MAGNETS

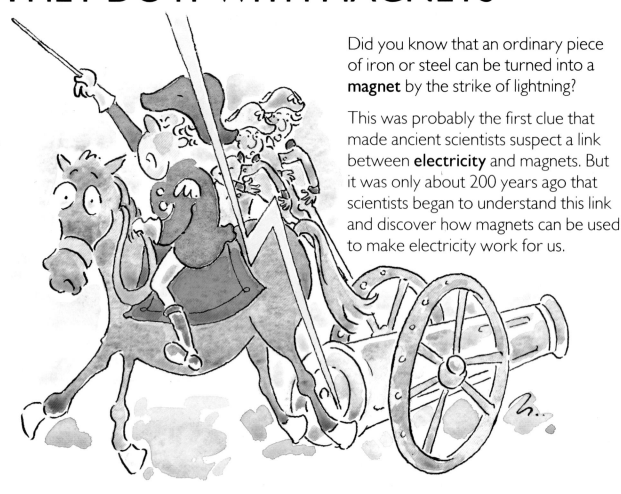

Did you know that an ordinary piece of iron or steel can be turned into a **magnet** by the strike of lightning?

This was probably the first clue that made ancient scientists suspect a link between **electricity** and magnets. But it was only about 200 years ago that scientists began to understand this link and discover how magnets can be used to make electricity work for us.

Electric motors work in just the opposite way to dynamos. Inside the motor, a coil of wire is held between the two ends of a magnet. When an electrical current flows through the coil of wire it spins round and round.

Electric motors can be made to do many things, but they all work by spinning round and round. And they all contain either a magnet or an electro-magnet.

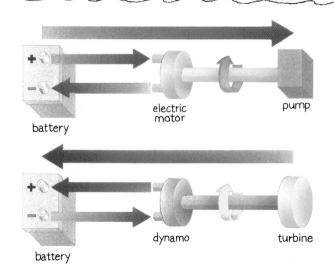

battery   electric motor   pump

battery   dynamo   turbine

Scrap metal yards use huge electro-magnets to pick up and move heavy objects made of iron and steel. To drop the load, the crane operator just shuts off the current.

Just as an electric current can make a magnet, a magnet can make an electrical current. Spinning a magnet or electro-magnet inside a coil of wire causes an electrical current to flow along the wire.

This is how the massive **electricity generators** inside power stations produce the powerful mains current that supplies our homes. It is also how a tiny dynamo works to produce the current to light up a bicycle lamp.

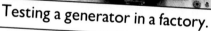
Testing a generator in a factory.

This roundabout and sewing machine both have an electric motor.

Brenda's day

My name is Brenda and I am the caretaker of St Ann's Special School in Morden, Surrey.

As soon as I arrive in the morning I go round checking the heating and equipment in the school. You'd be surprised how many different things use electricity in the school. I'm using it all day in my work – for instance I use this electric drill to put up a picture.

I often check the boiler. The pumps work by electricity. They pump hot water to the radiators all round the school.

Sylvia and Clive use computers, videos, and tape recorders in their classroom.

Playtime – Danny enjoys playing on the electric tricycle. There is a big battery under the seat.

Lorna is heating up the school dinners. The ovens work by electricity. The electric temperature probe in the little picture below works on a battery.

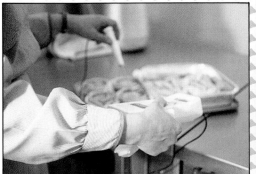

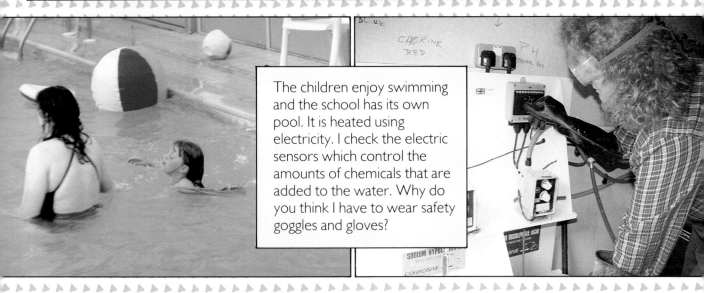

The children enjoy swimming and the school has its own pool. It is heated using electricity. I check the electric sensors which control the amounts of chemicals that are added to the water. Why do you think I have to wear safety goggles and gloves?

I started to make a list of everything in the school that works by electricity. You could make a list for your school.

swimming pool
fish tank
fire alarms
hair driers
computers
microwave
tricycle

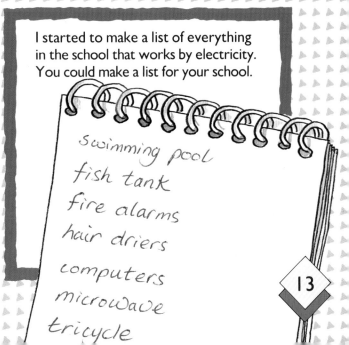

13

THE STORY OF MICHAEL FARADAY

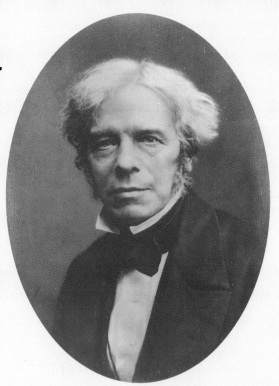

Michael Faraday was born in London in 1791. He grew up to become one of the world's most important scientists. The scientific discoveries he made changed the way people live. You can read about this on pages 7 and 17.

Only the children of rich people went to school when Michael Faraday was a child. He learned to read, write and do sums at his church Sunday school. The rest of the week he earned money delivering newspapers.

When Michael was 14, his boss decided to teach him how to bind books, a skill that would help him to get a good job when he was older. Michael read the books in his spare time. He found the science books most interesting.

One day, Michael went to see a famous scientist called Sir Humphry Davy give a talk at the Royal Institution. After that, Michael wanted more than anything else to help with scientific investigations at the Royal Institution's laboratories. He sent Sir Humphry a little book which he had bound himself containing the notes he'd made on the science talk. Sir Humphry invited Michael to visit him and offered him a job as a laboratory helper. Sir Humphry Davy made many scientific discoveries, but some people say that his most important discovery was Michael Faraday!

Michael Faraday wasn't just clever, he worked very hard and very long hours. He had a flat in the same building as the laboratory where he worked and when he got married, he and his wife shared a larger flat in the building.

He loved his work because he was curious about **magnets**, **electricity**, and other scientific puzzles. He didn't know that his discoveries would be put to so many good uses.

Scientific discoveries can also be put to bad uses; when the British government asked Michael to make poison gas to use as a weapon for war, he said no. He said it would be possible but that he wouldn't do it because it would be wrong.

Even though Michael Faraday was rather shy, he believed that he must share exciting news about scientific discoveries with the public. He thought it was most important to help children understand science. At Christmas time in 1826 he

gave several lectures at the Royal Institution that were especially for children. The Royal Institution has held Christmas Lectures for children ever since. Each year, children can come to see a famous scientist explain some of the latest scientific discoveries. Nowadays these lectures are broadcast on television so they can be seen by all children in Britain.

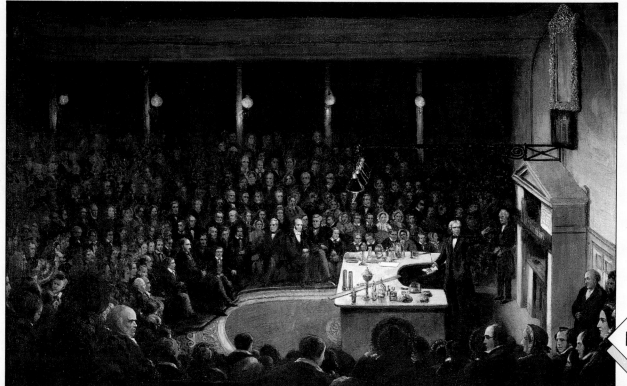

WHERE DOES THE MAINS CURRENT COME FROM?

Mains electrical current is generated by power stations like this one in Humberside. The current travels along cables away from the power station to homes, schools, factories and all other buildings in the area that are connected to the mains.

This power station is like a giant steam engine. Inside the station, coal is burned to heat water. The water boils and turns into steam.

Old steam railway engines transfer the power of the steam to turn the wheels of the engine. Power stations use it to turn **turbines**.

As the turbines spin they do something that Michael Faraday first did over a hundred and fifty years ago. Michael Faraday discovered that an electrical current would flow whenever he moved a magnet inside a coil of wire.

Today, all around the country, power station turbines are making our mains current flow by turning generators. In the generators powerful electro-magnets spin inside huge coils of wire.

Not all power stations burn coal to make steam. Some do it by burning oil or gas and others use **nuclear** energy.

Hydro-electric power stations do not use steam to make electricity. They use a fast flow of water to make the turbines spin. Much of Scotland's mains current flows from power stations like this one.

On the windy shore near Carmarthen, wind turbines supply electricity to homes in Dyfed. You can see a picture of one on page 19.

ELECTRICITY AND POLLUTION

Nowadays, using **electricity** is part of life. We need it for everything from traffic lights to incubators for premature babies. But we also need to keep the Earth's environment healthy. Will it be possible to keep both?

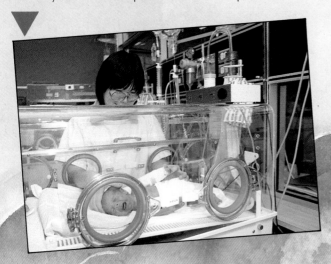

Most of the electricity we use in Britain today is made by burning fossil fuels such as coal, oil and gas. The main waste product of burning is a gas called carbon dioxide. It is normal for the Earth's air to contain carbon dioxide but burning fossil fuels is causing the amount of it to increase.

Many scientists believe this will cause the weather on the Earth to change. Some fear that the changes have already begun. The storms and droughts that have brought suffering to so many people in recent years may be partly due to the increase in carbon dioxide.

About a fifth of the electricity we use in Britain is generated in **nuclear** power stations. Some of the nuclear waste which they produce would be deadly if it escaped into the environment. The less dangerous waste used to be put into the sea in leakproof containers, but nowadays it is kept on site in purpose-built stores.

Specialized engineers working on the problem do their best to make sure that the waste doesn't escape, but accidents do happen, as at this power station in eastern Europe.

We also use the water power of flowing rivers to generate electricity and could use the tides in the same way.

The problem with using water power to make electricity is that it can destroy the natural habitat of the creatures that live in and around the water. If a hydro-electric power station were built on this estuary, these birds would be homeless.

Chernobyl, 1986

Many people believe we should make more use of wind power to produce electricity. But it would take more than a thousand wind **turbines** like this to generate the same amount of electricity as an average sized power station. Do you think people would be happy to see their environment filled with thousands and thousands of windmills?

LIGHTING A TELEVISION STUDIO

Have you noticed the list of names shown at the end of most television programmes? This long list only names a few of the people who helped to make the programme. If you keep a lookout at the end of BBC television programmes, you will probably see Duncan Brown's name. Duncan is a lighting director. 'The pictures on television only look right if the studio is properly lit. I work closely with directors and the people who design the scenery. Lighting helps to create the mood of a scene.

'In this programme, Terry Wogan will talk to some guests and one of the guests will sing. The guests sit and talk in a brightly lit part of the studio; the singer will be in a set which is darker and more dramatically lit.

'My job is artistic, but we also have to understand the technology involved. We have to know how to get the best out of the studio equipment and how to use it safely.

Duncan sends instructions from the studio floor to other members of the lighting team in the control room.

'It takes the whole day to rehearse and get the studio lighting ready for a programme that is broadcast in the evening. While my team adjusts the lights, the camera operators learn their positions.

'250 lights hang from the ceiling of the television studio, and we also use many more lights that stand on the floor.

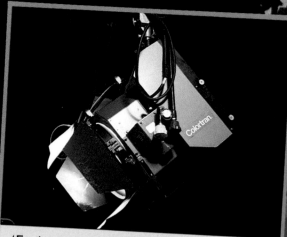

'Each studio light can be raised, lowered, tilted and turned. We can close doors to make sure the light only shines where we want it to shine. We can even pin coloured plastic on the front to make the light a different colour.

'In the lighting control room we study the pictures from each camera. All those knobs and dials are used for adjusting the colour and brightness of the pictures coming from each camera and controlling the strength of the electric current flowing to each light.

'The people who appear on television may be famous but they are only one part of a very large team.'

CLUES TO LIFE BEFORE ELECTRICITY

It was over 100 years ago that the first homes in Britain were connected to mains **electricity**. Very few people living in Britain today can remember what it was like to live without electricity but many of our best known stories, songs and rhymes are much older than electricity and they can give us clues to what life was like.

The story of Jack and the Beanstalk is an example. Do you remember the beginning of the story? Jack and his mother were so poor that they had sold everything except their cow. That's probably because, when the story of Jack and the Beanstalk was first told, a cow was the most useful thing a poor family could have. Keeping a cow was hard work but a family that owned one very rarely went hungry because it gave them fresh milk.

Milk comes from a cow at the cow's body temperature which is about 38°C. Nowadays we can cool the milk quickly and keep it fresh for several days in a fridge. Without one, milk quickly went off. It soon turned into yoghurt or curds and whey and after that, if they didn't do something, it would taste nasty.

People could preserve the goodness from milk by making it into cheese or butter. This took a long time and was hard work, but it gave the family a store of food to see them through the winter when grass doesn't grow and cows don't make much milk. Also, extra cheese and butter could be sold to people who didn't own a cow.

Today in Britain, a family doesn't have to own a cow to have fresh milk. Refrigeration keeps milk fresh so it can be transported and sold in shops. Few people even know how to milk a cow or turn the milk into cheese and butter. All the work is done for us. We can buy fresh milk, Longlife milk, tinned milk, and dried milk. We can also buy many different types of food that have been made from milk, such as cheese, butter, ice cream, yoghurt and other puddings.

If you go to a museum you may see things that people used in their homes before electricity.

Milking the cows at a modern dairy.

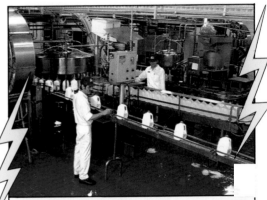

Bottling the milk.

Milk products for sale in a supermarket – this would be very difficult without electricity.

GLOSSARY

Battery
A store of electricity, from which you can draw an electric current whenever and wherever you need it.

Circuit
The path followed by an electric current. Usually a current will not cross an air gap, so a circuit cannot have a break in it.

This circuit is broken and the current will not flow.

Now the current is continuous all the way round and the current can flow.

Electricity
This is a special kind of energy. We use it for heating, lighting and working machines. It is produced in power stations and can be stored in batteries. When electricity moves from one place to another, we have an electric current.

Electricity generator
A machine that produces electricity. Some use heat, either from burning coal or gas or oil or from nuclear fuel. Others use the movement of wind or water.

Magnet
A piece of metal which attracts a piece of iron towards itself is called a magnet.

Nuclear
At the centre of every atom there is a small nucleus, which is a tiny storehouse of energy. This energy is called nuclear energy. The machines in a nuclear power station take some of this energy from atoms in the special nuclear fuel, and change it into electricity that we can use.

Turbine
A turbine is a machine that uses the movement of air or other gases, or of water, to turn a specially designed wheel called the rotor. Waterwheels and windmills are simple turbines. Power stations use large turbines with rotors that spin very fast indeed, to produce electricity.